GW01319670

Original title:
Frosted Lanterns

Author: Sabrina Sarvik
ISBN HARDBACK: 978-9916-79-687-0
ISBN PAPERBACK: 978-9916-79-688-7
ISBN EBOOK: 978-9916-79-689-4

Silhouetted Lights on a Winter's Eve

In the dusk of a quiet town,
Shadows dance with a silver gown.
Streetlamps flicker, a warm embrace,
As whispers of winter softly trace.

Snowflakes fall like gentle dreams,
Softly coating the moonlit beams.
Colors twinkle, the night ignites,
In the glow of silhouetted lights.

Children laughter fills the air,
Breath like clouds, a frosty flair.
Footsteps crunch on the snowy ground,
While secrets in the night abound.

Icicles hang like crystal tears,
Reflecting hopes through the years.
Every glow tells a tale untold,
Of warmth and joy against the cold.

As the stars in velvet skies gleam,
Winter's beauty feels like a dream.
With each heartbeat, the magic flows,
Underneath the sparkling snows.

Incandescence in Winter's Heart

In winter's chill, a fire glows,
A hidden warmth where stillness grows.
Frost-kissed branches softly sway,
Embers dance in twilight's play.

Beneath the stars, the darkness sighs,
With every spark, the silence flies.
A flicker bright, a calling spark,
Igniting hope within the dark.

Light Drifting on Icy Winds

Whispers ride on icy breath,
As daylight dances, teasing death.
Light drifts like snow through frozen air,
A fleeting moment, rare and fair.

In shadows cast by winter's hand,
A glowing warmth begins to stand.
It swirls and twirls, a gentle grace,
In every corner, warms the space.

Aurora Beneath the Silent Snow

Beneath the snow, a secret dreams,
Colors blend in soft moonbeams.
Auroras glow in ethereal lace,
While winter holds its quiet grace.

Silent night, the world alight,
With hues of violet, blue, and white.
Each shimmer sings, a tale untold,
Where whispered wishes freely unfold.

Shards of Light in a Frosted Realm

In frosted realms, the shards ignite,
Fragments gleam in pale moonlight.
Each crystal glitters, pure and bright,
A silent promise in the night.

With every breath, the winter sighs,
And mirrors back the tranquil skies.
In icy holds, the beauty's clear,
Shards of light draw loved ones near.

Frost-Kissed Memories Illuminate the Dark

Frost-kissed whispers haunt the night,
Memories dance in silver light.
Echoes linger in the air,
Soft reminders everywhere.

Shadows weave through trees so bare,
Time entangles with despair.
Footsteps crunch on frosty ground,
A heart's desire, longing found.

Through the chill, a spark ignites,
Lost moments grace the winter nights.
Layers deep in frost so white,
Illuminate the dark with light.

Halo of Light in a Wintry World

A halo shines in icy grace,
Cascading light, a warm embrace.
Snowflakes twirl on brisk, cold air,
Nature's art beyond compare.

Branches bow with laden snow,
In a world where dreams can grow.
Morning breaks with hues so bright,
Casting hope in purest light.

Each breath clouds in frosty air,
Whispers of dreams to softly share.
Around us, magic swirls anew,
In this wintry tale so true.

Crystalline Glow of the Quiet Dawn

Crystalline whispers greet the morn,
Awakening the world reborn.
In hushed tones, the day unfolds,
Stories of warmth, softly told.

Light dances on the frosted ground,
Nature's beauty all around.
The sky blushes in pastel hues,
Welcoming the day with muse.

Birdsong flutters through the trees,
Gentle echoes in the breeze.
With each ray, a promise given,
In the quiet, hearts are risen.

Ethereal Luster Beneath the Stars

Ethereal luster fills the night,
Stars like lanterns, oh so bright.
Cosmic whispers merge with dreams,
Flowing softly, like moonbeams.

Nighttime cloaks with velvet skies,
Dancing lights that mesmerize.
In this stillness, magic breeds,
A symphony of silent needs.

Underneath the starlit dome,
We find solace, find our home.
Every star a tale to tell,
In their glow, we weave our spell.

Celestial Fireflies in the Glistening Night

Tiny sparks dance in the air,
Whispers of magic everywhere.
Stars flicker, a gentle sight,
Celestial fireflies shine so bright.

In the garden, dreams take flight,
Chasing shadows, lost in light.
Through the realms of endless bliss,
Each twinkle reveals a wish.

Luminescent trails left behind,
Guided by the heart and mind.
Nature's jewels, pure delight,
In the embrace of tranquil night.

The Warmth of a Shimmering Remnant

Flickers of the fading day,
Soft embers of sun's last ray.
Hearts are warmed by the glow,
In stillness, memories flow.

Wrapped in comfort, shadows fade,
Each moment, sweetly made.
A shimmering remnant appears,
Filling the night with gentle cheers.

From ashes, hope finds its way,
Lighting paths where dreams may stay.
In the silence, whispers hum,
The warmth of love will always come.

Kaleidoscopes of Glow in the Void

In the vastness, colors blend,
Kaleidoscopes that twist and bend.
Mysteries swirl in quiet grace,
Finding patterns in empty space.

A dance of light, a cosmic play,
Illuminating the shades of gray.
Each bright hue, a story spun,
In the void, where shadows run.

With every gaze, secrets unfold,
Infinite wonders to behold.
Radiance bursts through the dark,
Each spark ignites a timeless spark.

Night's Tender Glow Between the Frost

Beneath the stars, the silence sighs,
Moonlit dreams weave through the skies.
A gentle warmth amidst the chill,
Night's tender glow, a quiet thrill.

Frosted fields mirror the light,
Dancing crystals, pure and white.
In the stillness, hearts ignite,
Embracing love on this clear night.

Soft whispers hush the autumn breeze,
In winter's grasp, a sense of ease.
Awakening souls, side by side,
Under the glow, we will abide.

Shards of Light in a Frozen Realm

In the stillness, whispers sing,
Frozen winds dance, joy they bring.
Shards of light, they pierce the night,
Glittering dreams in pure delight.

Crystals form on branches bare,
Nature's art beyond compare.
In the hush, a soft embrace,
Winter's touch, a fleeting grace.

Stars above in silence gleam,
Reflecting on a silver stream.
Each breath a cloud, a fleeting sigh,
In this realm, where moments fly.

Glistening Spheres of Winterscape

Glistening spheres on fields so white,
Nature's gems, a wondrous sight.
Beneath the moon, they softly glow,
Mirroring dreams from long ago.

Every flake, a story spun,
Whispers of warmth in the cold run.
Children laugh, their echoes clear,
In this realm, we hold so dear.

Footsteps crunch on frosted ground,
In the silence, joy is found.
Each moment captured, pure and bright,
In the canvas of the night.

Shivering Candles in the Gloom

Shivering candles flicker low,
Casting shadows, a warm glow.
In the dark, they softly sway,
Guiding hearts along the way.

Whispers dance on silent air,
Secrets held with gentle care.
Each flame a wish, a heartfelt plea,
In the twilight, wild and free.

Gloom retreats to their embrace,
Filling spaces with their grace.
Together in this fleeting light,
We find solace in the night.

Brightness Cast on Frosted Air

Brightness cast on frosted air,
Winter's kiss, a touch so rare.
Glowing paths in the early morn,
Nature's promise, softly sworn.

Trees adorned with icy lace,
Every branch a hidden space.
In the warmth of daylight's glow,
Magic whispers, soft and slow.

Clouds drift by, a painter's hand,
Sketching beauty across the land.
In this moment, hearts entwine,
Underneath the sun's design.

Brilliant Glows Amid Shivering Pines

In the forest, shadows sway,
Beneath the stars, the whispers play.
Pines stand tall, their secrets kept,
While brilliant glows around them crept.

Soft illumination fills the air,
Casting wonders everywhere.
Each flicker brings an endless tale,
As nature sings, the heart's set sail.

Moonlight dances on the leaves,
Twinkling softly as night weaves.
Amidst the woods, dreams touch the ground,
In every glimmer, joy is found.

Gentle breezes stir the night,
Guiding spirits into sight.
Brilliant glows in silver hues,
Illuminate the path we choose.

As dawn approaches, glows recede,
Yet in our hearts, they plant a seed.
The magic lingers, and we know,
In quiet woods, there's always a glow.

Ghostly Lights in the Winter Woods

Through the frozen, silent trees,
Whispers float on icy breeze.
Ghostly lights begin to show,
Dancing gently, soft and low.

Snowflakes twirl in the midnight dark,
Each shimmer holds a secret spark.
Nature's breath in winter's breath,
Lifeless trees, yet life bequeath.

Up above, the stars align,
Casting shadows, sharp and fine.
Crystals form on every bough,
Nature's artistry dressed in wow.

In the stillness, spirits glide,
With the moonlight as their guide.
Ghostly lights that twinkle bright,
Soothing the depths of the cold night.

The magic fades as dawn appears,
Yet in the heart, it reappears.
Ghostly lights in winter's wood,
Always felt, understood.

Radiance Dancing on Cold Streams

Where the river meets the night,
Radiance sparkles, soft and bright.
Rippling waters weave a tale,
Of dancing dreams in a silver veil.

Moonbeams kiss the frigid flow,
As gentle currents ebb and glow.
Each ripple tells the world to pause,
In silent wonder, nature's laws.

Branches dip to catch the light,
In the stillness, pure delight.
Radiance gleams on water's jest,
A tranquil heart, a spirit blessed.

Time stands still by the cold streams,
In this moment, life redeems.
Reflections shimmer, bring to mind,
The quiet beauty, pure and kind.

As night gives way to dawn's embrace,
Radiance fades without a trace.
Yet in our hearts, it lingers near,
The dance of light, forever dear.

Sparkling Guardians of the Night

In the dark, where silence reigns,
Sparkling lights break through the chains.
Guardians of the night take flight,
Bringing dreams adorned with light.

Stars above, like scattered gems,
Guard the world with ancient hems.
Each twinkle tells a tale of yore,
Of journeys made, of distant shores.

Whispers carried on the breeze,
Through the trees, among the leaves.
Sparkling guardians, brave and bold,
Keep watch over stories told.

Moonlit paths where shadows creep,
Safe they keep those fast asleep.
In the quiet, hearts take wing,
To the realm where nightingales sing.

As dawn arrives, the sparkles fade,
Yet in the soul, their mark is laid.
Sparkling guardians, bold and bright,
Forever shine in memory's light.

Illuminated Winter Whispers

Whispers of snow in the still night,
Gentle flakes dance, glimmering bright.
Moonlight spills on the frozen ground,
Softly breathing, a magic sound.

Trees adorned in a crystal glow,
Silver secrets in breezy flow.
Nature's sigh amidst winter's grace,
Lost in dreams, a tranquil space.

Footsteps muffled, serenity reigns,
Echoes of laughter like sweet refrains.
Frozen ponds, like mirrors, reflect,
Stories of ages, quiet, perfect.

Bare branches knit with icy lace,
Embracing the chill, a warm embrace.
Stars peek through in the velvet night,
Guiding hearts in the gentle light.

The air, crisp with a whispered refrain,
Holds promises sweet like soft champagne.
In winter's arms, all worries cease,
A world transformed, a realm of peace.

Glacial Lanterns of Serenity

Beneath a sky of cobalt blue,
Lanterns of ice, a magical view.
Frosty breath hangs in the air,
A dreamy realm, beyond compare.

Fields of white, where silence blooms,
Nature's beauty, in winter's rooms.
Each crystal flake tells a tale,
Of fleeting moments, soft and frail.

Whispers echo through the trees,
Carried softly on chilling breeze.
Every rustle, a lover's touch,
A symphony played, oh so much.

Glistening pathways through the night,
Leading hearts with twinkling light.
Moonbeams sparkle on tranquil lakes,
Reflecting dreams, where hope awakes.

In this kingdom where wonder thrives,
The spirit of winter forever jives.
With glacial lamps lighting the way,
Serenity reigns, come what may.

Chilled Radiance in the Stillness

In the hush of a starry eve,
Radiance glows, as we believe.
Chilled whispers float beyond the dark,
Each sparkle sings, a gentle lark.

Blankets of snow, a soft embrace,
Nature's art in a tranquil space.
Frozen rivers, still as a dream,
Reflecting glimmers, a soft gleam.

The world sleeps under moon's caress,
Wrapped in peace, no need for stress.
Crisp air fills lungs, sparking delight,
Hearts beat softly in the night.

Frost-kissed windows frame the view,
A masterpiece where magic brews.
Every shadow tells a tale,
Of warmth within the winter's veil.

So let us wander through this scene,
In stillness found, where hearts convene.
Chilled radiance, a wondrous sight,
Guides us home through the endless night.

Twinkling Frost upon the Breeze

Twinkling frost in the morning light,
Covers the earth in sheer delight.
Delicate patterns, nature's lace,
Awakening the sleepy grace.

Each breath a cloud in the crisp air,
A moment of joy, beyond compare.
Sunrise sparkles on the glazed trees,
Whispering dreams in a gentle breeze.

Footsteps crunch on a winter's morn,
Echoes of laughter, sweetly born.
Nature's canvas, pure and bright,
Capturing hearts in its light.

With every glance, a world unveiled,
Stories of beauty, softly sailed.
Frosty tendrils, a delicate touch,
Embrace the spirit, oh so much.

Hold this feeling in your heart's core,
Let it linger forevermore.
For in the chill, we find a spark,
Twinkling frost ignites the dark.

Morning Glow on Icy Slopes

The sun peeks over peaks,
Casting light on icy creeks.
A halo of warmth starts to grow,
Morning glow on the slopes below.

Frosty crystals sparkle bright,
Glimmers dance in morning light.
Footprints crunch on snow so bright,
Nature's canvas, pure delight.

Birds call from distant trees,
Whispers carried on the breeze.
A tranquil hush, the world awakes,
In harmony, the silence breaks.

Trees stand tall, cloaked in white,
A winter wonder, pure and right.
Each flake a gem in sun's embrace,
A fleeting moment, time and space.

In this realm of cold and grace,
Life's magic finds its place.
Morning's brush paints all anew,
On icy slopes, a vibrant hue.

Lanterns of Luster Amidst the Frost

Flickering lights in the night,
Lanterns glimmer, soft and bright.
Casting warmth through bitter cold,
Stories of winter gently told.

Snowflakes tumble from above,
Each one kissed with winter's love.
Beneath the glow, shadows play,
Whispers of light guide the way.

The world wrapped in a silken sheet,
Nature's slumber, soft and sweet.
Lanterns sway on icy posts,
Guardians of dreams, gentle hosts.

Footfalls echo through the hush,
Time slows down, heartbeats rush.
Amidst the frost, a vibrant scene,
Magic weaves through every dream.

With each step, the night ignites,
Illuminated tales take flight.
Lanterns shine with tales of old,
In frosty air, warmth unfolds.

The Chill of a Thousand Stars

In the night, the cold winds blow,
Stars twinkle in a dazzling show.
Each one shines a silver hue,
Whispering secrets old and true.

The chill wraps round, a soft embrace,
In this celestial, endless space.
Beneath the vast and starlit dome,
Hearts wander through the cosmos, home.

Winter's breath fills the crisp air,
Those sparkling gems, beyond compare.
Gaze upward, let your spirit soar,
Amongst the stars, find evermore.

A quiet peace settles in tight,
Wrapped in the magic of the night.
With every star, a wish takes flight,
The chill of a thousand stars so bright.

In silence, dreams begin to rise,
Under the watch of starlit skies.
A cosmic dance, a wondrous art,
Each twinkle plays a vital part.

Glowing Recommendations of Winter

The scent of pine fills the air,
As winter blankets everywhere.
Fires crackle, warmth unfolds,
Glowing stories silently told.

Mittens snug on tiny hands,
Steamy cups on frosted stands.
Laughter echoes under the moon,
Winter nights sing a sweet tune.

Snowmen stand with smiles so wide,
Children play with hearts open wide.
Each flake falls in joyful cheer,
Nature whispers, winter is here.

Candles flicker, shadows dance,
In the stillness, hearts advance.
Puzzles shared and tales recited,
In glowing warmth, lives ignited.

Embrace the chill, the shining glow,
Let love and laughter overflow.
For in this season, joys we find,
Glow with warmth, hearts intertwined.

Glittering Shadows of the Cold

In midnight's clutch, the shadows creep,
Their whispers soft, secrets they keep.
A dance of frost on the silent ground,
Beneath the stars, no echoes found.

Glistening trails of silver hue,
Twinkling softly, a muted view.
Cold winds sigh as they sweep along,
In nature's clasp, we all belong.

Frosted branches arch and bend,
Embracing cold, no need to fend.
With every breath, a crystal gleam,
In shadows deep, we chase a dream.

The moonlit path, a guiding light,
Where shadows weave through endless night.
In the glittering realms, we find our way,
To warm the heart till break of day.

A symphony in the chill we hear,
The whispered tales when night draws near.
With every twinkle, each muted sigh,
We chase the shadows, the cold sky high.

Radiant Dreams in Icebound Nights

When moonbeams dance on frosted eaves,
Radiant dreams weave through the leaves.
In frozen realms where wishes spark,
We gather hope, igniting the dark.

The universe twirls in icy grace,
As shadows slip from their resting place.
Every heartbeat sends sparks anew,
In tranquil nights, all dreams come true.

Icicles hold a crystal glow,
Fractured light in the deepened snow.
In this enchanting, frozen embrace,
We find our warmth, our resting space.

Whispers linger on the frigid air,
As stars glitter in dreams we share.
Through icebound nights, our spirits soar,
Bound by starlight, forever more.

In the silence, our hearts entwine,
Each radiant dream, a sacred sign.
Amidst the cold, love's warmth ignites,
In the magic of those icebound nights.

Whispering Lights in the Snow

Beneath the quiet, there lies a hum,
Whispering lights, oh, how they come.
In the shimmering white, they softly gleam,
Guiding us through a frosty dream.

With every flake, a story spun,
A journey shared 'neath the winter sun.
Each twinkling spark, a fleeting sound,
In this serene world, peace is found.

The night unfolds in a spectral glow,
Casting spells on the silent snow.
Radiant beams dance with delight,
A tapestry woven in soft moonlight.

Crystalline visions float and weave,
In whispered tales, we believe.
As snowflakes fall, they bear a song,
In this enchanted realm, we belong.

With every breeze, the magic thrives,
Whispering lights where wonder drives.
In winter's grip, our souls ignite,
Amidst the snow, our hearts take flight.

Clusters of Light Amidst the Frost

Clusters of light in the frosty air,
Speckled stars in the night we share.
With each glimmer, a story unfolds,
In winter's breath, the silence holds.

A blanket of white, serene and still,
The world sleeps beneath a dreamer's will.
Each dazzling flicker, a soft embrace,
In the night's calm, we find our place.

Crystals twinkle like distant beams,
Reflecting hopes, igniting dreams.
In the shadowy corners, memories flow,
Clusters of light in the softening snow.

With whispers shared, we venture forth,
Carrying warmth from the hearth of worth.
Amongst the cold, our spirits gleam,
In the frosty night, we dare to dream.

The sky spills secrets, gleaming bright,
Clusters of wonder pierce the night.
As thoughts entwine and hearts keep beat,
In this frosted realm, our lives are sweet.

Shimmering Stars Beneath the Snow

Whispers of frost on the ground,
Stars in silence can be found.
Each flake dances in the light,
Twinkling softly through the night.

Glistening gems on a quilted sheet,
Nature's beauty, pure and sweet.
Cold air wraps a hushed embrace,
Dreams of winter's tranquil grace.

Beneath the moon's ethereal glow,
Lies a world draped in snow.
Together, shadows gently play,
As night turns slowly into day.

Footsteps crunch on frozen ground,
Silent wonders all around.
In the stillness, hearts align,
With the stars, forever shine.

Among the drifts, still and deep,
Nature sings the songs of sleep.
Underneath this quiet sky,
Shimmering secrets softly lie.

Frost-Crowned Chasers of the Dark

In the night where shadows creep,
Frost-crowned dreams begin to seep.
Chasers of the winter air,
Hopes and whispers linger there.

Lights that flicker, faint and bright,
Dance like fireflies in the night.
Through the chill, we roam afar,
Searching for a guiding star.

Breath like steam in crisp, cool air,
Every moment, pure and rare.
Upon the ground, so frozen still,
Lies a landscape, wild and real.

Hushed beneath a velvety sky,
A tranquil world that we can't deny.
Frosty fingers gently trace,
The beauty of this cold embrace.

As dawn approaches, shadows flee,
Chasing light, wild and free.
Like shooting stars that break the dark,
In their wake, we leave our mark.

Celestial Glow in Hushed Wilderness

In deep woods where silence reigns,
Celestial glow softly wanes.
Stars like lanterns guide our way,
Through the night until the day.

Branches whisper tales untold,
Wrapped in silver, blue, and gold.
In this calm, the heart does soar,
Every breath reveals much more.

Underneath the constellation,
Nature sings in celebration.
Softly cradled by the night,
Glowing wonders, pure delight.

Flickers caught in the breeze,
Whispers float among the trees.
In this sanctuary so vast,
Moments linger, memories last.

When the dawn begins to break,
Wilderness stirs, and we awake.
In the quiet, love remains,
In the light, the heart regains.

Twinkling Lights in Silent Frost

Twinkling lights in a world of frost,
Every shimmer, something lost.
As stillness blankets all around,
Magic joins the whispered sound.

Underneath the icy dome,
Far away, the stars call home.
With each breath, the night expands,
Holding dreams within its hands.

Footsteps echo on the trail,
In the silence, hearts exhale.
Frosty air and glowing skies,
Promise of the dawn that lies.

Every sparkle tells a tale,
Of adventures without fail.
The night is young, and hope is bright,
In this world of purest light.

With the morning, all will change,
Yet these moments feel so strange.
In the frost, our spirits play,
Chasing warmth through light of day.

Frosted Dreams of Nocturnal Bliss

In the still of night we wander,
Through the realms of frost and chill,
Stars above us softly ponder,
Whispers of our hearts fulfill.

With a sigh, the snowflakes dance,
Blanketing the world in white,
In this world, we find our chance,
To dream beneath the moonlight bright.

Frozen laughter fills the air,
Echoes of the past we chase,
In this moment, free from care,
Time stands still in time and space.

The trees are draped in silver sheen,
Nature's canvas, pure and grand,
Crystals spark with glow unseen,
Painting dreams upon the land.

In our hearts, the warmth ignites,
Frosted dreams of love abide,
Together in the starry nights,
In laughter, joy, and bliss, we bide.

Whispers of Luminosity in the Snow

Underneath the pale moonlight,
Snowflakes glisten, whispers low,
Every flake a kiss of light,
Gentle paths where dreamers go.

Veiled in white, a world asleep,
Secrets wrapped in snowy shrouds,
Through the silence, soft and deep,
Whispers dance as night en clouds.

Stars are watching from their home,
Guiding us with silver beams,
In the dark, we softly roam,
Chasing each other's fleeting dreams.

Echoes of a distant chime,
Through the stillness, softly flow,
In this moment, frozen time,
Whispers weave through drifts of snow.

Awake to the dawn's embrace,
Colors bloom in morning light,
Yet forever in this space,
Whispers linger through the night.

Flickering Spirits Beneath the Frost

In the quiet, shadows play,
Flickering like candle flames,
Beneath the frost, they sway,
Dancing softly, calling names.

Ghostly figures in the night,
Whirls of mist upon the ground,
In their glow, we find the light,
Whispers echo all around.

In the hush, a story told,
Of the spirits, lost yet free,
Through the frost, they softly scold,
Guardians of our memories.

Twinkling stars in velvet skies,
Lend their glow to fleeting dreams,
In their gaze, our hopes arise,
In the frost, the spirit gleams.

So we wander, hand in hand,
Through this realm of dreams and light,
Feeling magic, soft and grand,
Flickering spirits guide the night.

Glimmering Horizons of Stillness

Where the earth and sky converge,
Glimmering horizons unfold,
In the stillness, hearts emerge,
Stories of the brave and bold.

The quiet air, a gentle balm,
Calming every restless thought,
In this space, we find our calm,
Embracing all that we have sought.

Snow-kissed peaks embrace the dawn,
Illuminated by soft light,
A new day gently drawn,
In this beauty, our souls take flight.

Every breath a treasure shared,
With the world, a sacred bond,
In this peace, we feel unware,
Of the chaos that's beyond.

So let us stand and take a gaze,
At the glimmering horizon's kiss,
In this moment, lost in praise,
We find our stillness in pure bliss.

Sigils of Light on a Frozen Sea

Beneath the icy veil of night,
Stars weave patterns, bold and bright.
A frozen sea reflects the glow,
Of ancient sigils, tales from long ago.

Whispers carried on the breeze,
Each symbol holds a mystery.
The light dances on the waves,
Illuminating secrets, deep in caves.

Hushed are the echoes of the past,
As shadows flicker, flicker fast.
In beauty's arms, we find our peace,
Time stands still, our thoughts release.

The night consumes the fleeting day,
Yet hope remains in light's soft sway.
On frozen seas, our hearts unite,
In the shimmering sigils of the night.

Dance of the Shimmering Night

The moon spills silver on the ground,
In every shadow, magic found.
Stars twinkle as the night takes flight,
A tapestry woven, pure delight.

Crickets serenade the cool air,
While fireflies flicker with gentle flair.
Each moment breathes a rhythmic tune,
A dance of whispers beneath the moon.

The breeze weaves through the trees so tall,
Carrying secrets, a soft enthrall.
In this embrace, we sway and spin,
A waltz of dreams, where love begins.

Sparkling moments cascade like rain,
In this shimmering night, we feel no pain.
The world fades into a soft embrace,
As we lose ourselves in time and space.

Secrets Wrapped in Frost

Morning breaks with a frozen sigh,
The world is draped in a crystal lie.
Each leaf and branch encased in white,
Hiding stories of the night.

Nature whispers through frosty air,
Secrets linger everywhere.
Yet in the cold, a warmth does glow,
Tender tales only few will know.

With every breath, a cloud of dreams,
Reflecting light in silver streams.
In the stillness, magic stirs,
In forgotten words, the mystery blurs.

Frosted whispers, silent, strong,
Echo memories that linger long.
In this realm of winter's grace,
Secrets wrapped in nature's embrace.

Frosty Echoes in the Dark

In the dark, the frost does cling,
Silent whispers, shadows sing.
Echoes dance on the icy ground,
Nature's secrets, softly found.

Stars blink gently, a midnight call,
While winter's breath covers all.
A chilling beauty, stark and bold,
In this hush, the stories unfold.

Moonlight bathes the world in peace,
While time drifts slowly, thoughts release.
Frosty echoes in silent grace,
Guide us through this tranquil space.

With every step, a fleeting trace,
Of laughter lost in winter's embrace.
In the dark, the frost will stay,
Glimmers of light along the way.

Celestial Glow Amidst the Chill

In the quiet of night, stars gleam so bright,
Moonlight dances softly, a soothing sight.
Whispers of winter, they glide and sway,
Nature's heart beats gently, in a cool, sweet play.

Frosted branches shimmer, a diamond lace,
Each breath we take, a cloud in the space.
Chilled winds carry secrets, stories untold,
Wrapped in warm silence, the world feels bold.

Glimmers of hope in the darkest hour,
Beneath the starlit sky, we feel the power.
Journey through shadows, with dreams in tow,
Embrace the night's magic, let your heart glow.

As the dawn creeps in, colors arise,
A palette of warmth, the sun's sweet surprise.
Celestial visions fade, but softly stay,
The chill of the night gives way to the day.

Crystalline Reflections on Hidden Trails

Winding paths whisper secrets long buried,
Nature's embrace where silence is revered.
Crystals of rain on leaves intertwine,
Each droplet glistening, a moment divine.

Underfoot, soft moss, a comforting bed,
Footprints of wanderers, where stories have led.
Rustling leaves echo, a melodic sound,
Every turn taken, a treasure is found.

Glacial lakes mirror the sky's endless blue,
Ripples of memories flash anew.
Breezes that carry the scent of the past,
In this serene haven, time moves so fast.

Hidden trails guide us to places unknown,
Crystalline beauty, a realm overgrown.
With each step forward, the journey unfolds,
A dance with the wild, where the heart feels bold.

Pilgrimage of the Shining Beacons

From mountain tops high, to valleys below,
We walk in silence where warm breezes blow.
Fires flicker softly, a guiding light,
Promises of hope through the endless night.

Each beacon a story, a life that has passed,
Wisdom of ages, in memories cast.
Hands clasped in prayer, beneath the vast sky,
Together we journey, with spirits high.

The glow of the lanterns, a dance of the brave,
Embers of courage, our souls they save.
Chasing the twilight, we're not alone,
Every step taken, leads us back home.

As dawn paints horizons with hues of gold,
The pilgrimage whispers, its tales to be told.
In the arms of the light, we find our path clear,
Warmed by the beacons, we conquer our fear.

Candescent Wonders in the Stillness

In the hush of the dusk, the world takes a breath,
Candescent wonders bloom, defying death.
Flickers of magic in the cool evening air,
Every heartbeat whispers, a moment so rare.

The glow of the fire, as shadows play long,
Harmony lingers, a soft, soothing song.
Familiar faces gathered, sharing delight,
In the warmth of this stillness, our spirits take flight.

Stars blink above, like eyes watching wide,
The night holds us close, in its tender stride.
Dreams unravel slowly, in this golden hue,
Candescent wonders weave tales tried and true.

As the night deepens, our laughter rings clear,
Bonds forged in the stillness, our hearts draw near.
With every shared moment, we grow and ignite,
In this canvas of darkness, we bring forth the light.

Enchanted Glow of Winter's Breath

Beneath the silvered trees, they dance,
Whispers of snowflakes hold their chance.
Frosted whispers in the still of night,
A world aglow, bathed in soft white.

Winter wraps the earth in a gentle sigh,
Stars break through the velvet sky.
In this serene, enchanted bliss,
Frozen moments, too sweet to miss.

Fires crackle with a warm embrace,
As shadows waltz, we find our place.
Memories twirl, like leaves in the breeze,
Captured in time, hearts filled with ease.

Softly now, the night begins to fade,
With every breath, a promise made.
The glow of winter, pure and bright,
Guides us gently to morning light.

As dawn arrives, the world awakes,
Nature's art through the silence breaks.
In the enchanted glow, we believe,
Winter's breath, a magic we weave.

Echoes of the Frosted Twilight

Twilight whispers secrets of the cold,
In shimmering silence, stories unfold.
Shadows cast by the fading sun,
Echoes of warmth, the day is done.

Beneath a blanket, white and deep,
Dreams of winter gently creep.
Frosted memories in every breath,
Life dances softly with the death.

Silver moonlight spills on frozen ground,
In this twilight, solace is found.
Stillness reigns where laughter played,
Moments cherished, shall never fade.

Branches glisten in the evening's glow,
As dreams take flight like wings of snow.
Each heartbeat echoes in the night,
A symphony of pure delight.

With every glance towards the sky,
Winter's beauty makes the heart sigh.
In the frosted twilight, we find grace,
A whispered promise of a warm embrace.

Luminescence beneath the Ice

In the crystal depths, a magic lies,
Luminescent dreams beneath the skies.
Flashes of color in the icy sea,
Nature's wonders, wild and free.

Reflections dance on the frozen lake,
Whispers of life within the wake.
Branches draped in a silvery sheen,
Breathe in the beauty, serene and keen.

Flickering lights in the winter's hush,
Calling forth the night's gentle rush.
A tranquil stillness, peace so rare,
Within this winter's whispered prayer.

Underneath the ice, a glow remains,
Life's essence flows through frozen veins.
With every layer, each story told,
The warmth of heart and spirit bold.

As the sun dips low, where shadows will play,
The luminescence guides our way.
A beacon bright beneath the cold,
Winter's magic, timeless and bold.

Dreams Light Years from Hearth

In the quiet night, dreams take flight,
Wanderlust calls beneath the starlight.
Imaginary lands lie far and wide,
See the worlds where hopes abide.

A hearth so warm, yet distant it seems,
Animated lives within our dreams.
Journeys beckon, whispers of fate,
Adventure waits, but we hesitate.

Fireside glows with tales of old,
But in our hearts, young spirits unfold.
Through windows of time, we find our way,
Chasing horizons at break of day.

Every flicker tells a story anew,
Voices echo of journeys we pursue.
In the night's embrace, we find our part,
Carrying dreams that light the heart.

With every breath, we yearn and strive,
Through realms of wonder, our spirits thrive.
Dreams light years from the hearth so dear,
Ignite the spark, chase away the fear.

Brilliant Frost on Twilight's Edge

On the brink of nightfall's grace,
A sparkle glints on nature's face.
Whispers of winter lightly tread,
Painting a canvas, soft and spread.

Each blade of grass wears a crown,
Glistening bright, no hint of frown.
As shadows grow, the colors shift,
A fleeting moment, a precious gift.

The air grows crisp, as silence falls,
Nature listens to the twilight calls.
Brilliant frost, a shimmering lace,
Embraces earth in a cold embrace.

Stars awaken in the dusky hue,
While icy breath whispers anew.
The world transforms with a silent shout,
Brilliant frost, what it's all about.

Another night, another chance to see,
The beauty that sets our spirits free.
Under the moonlight, visions roam,
In the heart of winter, we find our home.

Nighttime Diamonds in Hazy Whisper

In the cloak of the night so deep,
Diamonds twinkle, secrets to keep.
Hazy whispers dance on the breeze,
A gentle sigh among the trees.

Moonlight spills on the tranquil lake,
Soft secrets that the shadows make.
Each flicker tells a story well,
Of dreams and wishes, a silent spell.

A tapestry woven with radiant spark,
Lighting up the serene, quiet dark.
The hush of night, a tender embrace,
Wrapped in wonder, time slows its pace.

Stars cascade like silver rain,
Each drop a note in a soft refrain.
As night unfolds, the world ignites,
Glittering gems in the tranquil nights.

In this magic, our hearts take flight,
Carried by diamonds in the night.
In hazy whispers, we find our place,
Beneath the stars, in endless grace.

Shining Fortunes in Snowbound Stillness

In fields of white, the silence reigns,
Snowbound beauty, pure remains.
Fortunes shining, a timeless glow,
Wrapped in stillness, deep below.

Winter's quilt, a soft and warm,
Hiding wonders in its charm.
Each flake a treasure, unique to see,
Falling gently, wild and free.

Tree branches bow, a graceful bend,
With every gust, the snow will send.
Shining fortunes, nature's grace,
In the heart of winter's embrace.

The world hushed in frosty sighs,
Reflects the dreams of endless skies.
Each moment captured, tranquil and bright,
In snowbound stillness, everything's right.

As twilight fades to a starry black,
Fortunes gleam, no hope we lack.
In the calm of night, our hearts are still,
Embracing magic, an endless thrill.

Frosted Dreams in Crystal Clarity

Frosted dreams dance on the air,
In crystal clarity, without a care.
Nature whispers in a voice so light,
Revealing wonders in the night.

Each breath a cloud, a moment held,
Stories of winter quietly spelled.
With every shimmer, a tale unfolds,
Of glowing hearts and dreams untold.

The world reflects in silvery sheen,
A diamond light on a frigid scene.
In frosted dreams, our wishes soar,
Hearts entwined, we crave for more.

Amidst the chill, a warmth inside,
In crystal clarity, we confide.
Every flake a promise to embrace,
Frosted dreams in a gentle grace.

As night deepens, our hopes ignite,
Guided by starlight's softest light.
Frosted dreams, both near and far,
Crystal clarity, our guiding star.

Enigmatic Gleam at Dawn

Misty whispers greet the light,
As stars fade into day so bright.
Shadows dance with soft embrace,
Awakening the world with grace.

Golden rays pierce through the haze,
Painting skies in vibrant blaze.
Nature stirs with gentle sighs,
As morning breaks and hope will rise.

Birds take flight with joyful song,
A melody that feels so strong.
Each note carries dreams anew,
In the dawn's soft, tender hue.

Leaves shimmer with dew's delight,
Glistening jewels in morning light.
A fleeting moment, pure and clear,
Hushed in beauty, wide and near.

The world awakens, full of grace,
In every heart, a sacred space.
With every breath, we start anew,
Embraced by dawn's enchanting view.

Opalescent Dreams in Chill

Frosted air bites at the skin,
Where twilight whispers soft, begin.
In shades of blue and silver gleam,
We wander through a waking dream.

Stars drip down like melting snow,
As winter's breath begins to flow.
Each moment draped in icy lace,
In opalescent calm we trace.

The world transforms, a wonderland,
With every flake that graces land.
They twirl and swirl like memories,
In the hush of freezing breeze.

Crisp as whispers, sharp as thought,
In frozen realms, our hearts are caught.
The chill ignites our deepest dreams,
In the glow of moonlit beams.

Night unfolds like velvet soft,
While distant echoes gently loft.
In every breath, a magic feeds,
Opalescent dreams plant tender seeds.

Charmed Lights on Winter's Frontier

Twinkling stars on snowy hills,
Whispers dance with winter chills.
The night adorned in silver threads,
A tapestry where magic spreads.

Each breath a cloud in frosty air,
As shadows linger everywhere.
The moonlight casts a gentle plight,
On winter's canvas, pure delight.

Footprints mark our wandering path,
In silent woods that stir the wrath.
Softly, softly, the world lies still,
Magnetic pull, a gentle thrill.

Crystal branches, nature's lace,
Woven dreams in frozen space.
A fleeting glance, a whisper shared,
In charmed lights, hearts laid bare.

Whispers sing of nights divine,
In every moment, love will shine.
Together, we find warmth anew,
On winter's frontier, just us two.

The Lure of the Icy Glow

In twilight's hush, the night unfolds,
A shimmering story quietly told.
Frosted air, a breath of sighs,
Underneath the starry skies.

Crystals dance in moon's embrace,
Illuminating every space.
With icy glow, the world transforms,
As nature weathers coldest storms.

Echoes linger in the still,
Promises of an evening thrill.
Each spark ignites a hidden wish,
In the chill, a fleeting bliss.

Hearts alight with fervent dreams,
Underneath the silver beams.
In icy realms where shadows play,
We find the magic on display.

As night prevails, we draw each breath,
Embraced by beauty, life, and depth.
The lure of glow that starts to show,
Captivates our souls in flow.

Chasing the Specters of Light

In the dawn, shadows play soft,
Whispers of dreams in skies aloft.
With every step, a gleam we chase,
Across the world, in time and space.

Ghostly figures dance on air,
Flickering sparks of the things we dare.
They guide us through the moment's haze,
Leading our hearts to brighter days.

Beneath the stars, the night unfolds,
Stories of wonder, quietly told.
We reach for hopes, with hands outstretched,
In each small flicker, we're enmeshed.

Through the shadows, our laughter rings,
As we wander where the twilight clings.
Chasing specters, forever bright,
Lost in the dance of fleeting light.

From dusk till dawn, our spirits soar,
The echoes of light, forever more.
In every heartbeat, we find our song,
Chasing the specters, where we belong.

Beacons Against the Winter's Veil

In winter's chill, the fires burn,
Against the frost, our hearts will yearn.
With every flame, a story shared,
Of warmth and love, forever bared.

Through snowy nights, the beacons shine,
Illuminating paths, for yours and mine.
In silence deep, their glow persists,
A promise held in the cold mists.

The howling wind may chill the air,
Yet hope and light will always dare.
For every shadow, there's a gleam,
A spark to warm the coldest dream.

We gather close, in shared embrace,
Finding comfort in this sacred space.
Together we stand, brave and strong,
Against the winter, where we belong.

As snowflakes dance, our spirits rise,
With every twinkle in the skies.
Beacons aglow, guiding our way,
Through winter's veil, to brighter days.

Spheres of Radiance in the Night

In the dark, stars twinkle bright,
Casting whispers of purest light.
Each sphere a promise, shining clear,
In the vastness, we draw near.

Galaxies spin in cosmic tides,
Where mysteries of beauty resides.
With open hearts, we gaze above,
Finding the magic, we all love.

Through the silence, a soft embrace,
Spheres of radiance, time won't erase.
Journeys unfold in celestial grace,
Guiding us home to a sacred place.

Every flicker tells a tale,
Of distant worlds where dreams set sail.
In this canvas, our hopes ignite,
Spheres of wonder in the night.

With every glance towards the skies,
We chase the visions, where truth lies.
In the universe, we find our might,
Among the spheres of radiant light.

Glimmers of the Enchanted Breeze

In the meadow, whispers hum,
Softly calling, the world succumb.
Glimmers dance on petals fair,
Carried sweetly through the air.

The breeze, a melody so light,
Plays with shadows, a joyful sight.
Each flutter brings a tale anew,
Of dreams awakened, and skies of blue.

Through the trees, the secrets flow,
In every rustle, the soft winds blow.
A gentle sigh, a breezy tease,
Glimmers weave through the enchanted trees.

In twilight's hue, the magic grows,
Lighting paths where soft light glows.
Through every whisper, hearts will tease,
Finding comfort in the enchanted breeze.

So let us wander, hand in hand,
In this realm, where dreams expand.
With every glance and every squeeze,
We'll chase the glimmers in the breeze.

Winter's Glistening Glow

Snowflakes drift, like whispers soft,
Blanketing the earth so loft.
Trees stand tall, with branches bare,
Sparkling jewels, hanging in the air.

Fireplaces crackle, warmth inside,
While winter winds in silence glide.
Hot cocoa steams in mugs held tight,
As stars emerge in frosty night.

Time slows down, in this still scene,
Nature rests, calm and serene.
Footprints left on glistening trails,
Tell the stories of winter's tales.

Moonlight dances on icy streams,
Reflecting softly on our dreams.
Each breath rises in frosty puffs,
Whispering secrets of winter huffs.

Together we gather, hearts align,
In this glistening glow, love we find.
Moments cherished, wrapped in light,
As winter graces us with its sight.

Crystal Beacons in the Night

Stars twinkle high, like crystal beacons,
Guiding the lost, where hope beacon.
In the quiet of a frosty eve,
Nature's magic, hard to believe.

Snowdrifts whisper tales of old,
Dreams embroidered in silver and gold.
The moon casts shadows, soft and pale,
As time stands still, we wander the trail.

Icicles hang like fragile dreams,
Catching light in gleaming beams.
Whispers of wind, secrets untold,
In the heart of winter, brave and bold.

Candles flicker, warm and bright,
Childhood memories in the night.
Every light a story spun,
Of laughter shared and love begun.

Wrapped in blankets, we gaze above,
Counting stars, renewing love.
In this stillness, peace we find,
Crystal beacons, forever entwined.

Shimmering Echoes of December

December's chill bites at the air,
Shimmers softly, everywhere.
Each breath a cloud, drifting slow,
In the hush of winter's glow.

Frosted windows with intricate lace,
Nature's artist, with gentle grace.
Carols echo, sweet and clear,
Filling hearts with winter cheer.

Footsteps crunch on snowy ground,
With each movement, magic found.
Whispers of joy, laughter rings,
Celebrating love that winter brings.

Glistening paths lead to distant dreams,
Where light dances and hope redeems.
Under the eaves, the snowflakes sway,
Telling stories in their own way.

As night descends, shadows play,
In shimmering echoes, we softly stay.
Wrapped in warmth, the fire glows,
Embracing winter's tender throws.

Frost's Embrace on Shining Orbs

Morning light breaks through the trees,
Kissing frost in the gentle breeze.
Nature sparkles, a jeweled show,
In frost's embrace, magic flows.

Crystalline patterns weave through time,
Each breath a whisper, in silent rhyme.
Snowflakes glisten, twirling down,
Crowning the earth in a silver gown.

Joyful laughter, children play,
Building dreams in winter's sway.
Each snowman stands, proud and tall,
As evening falls, they greet us all.

Stars awaken in the night,
Shining orbs, a pure delight.
Whirling above in cosmic dance,
Winter's magic holds us in trance.

Together we share this frosty charm,
Wrapped in warmth, safe from harm.
In nature's hush, our spirits rise,
Frost's embrace, under starlit skies.

Winter's Emissaries of Light

Snowflakes dance in the pale moonlight,
Whispers of magic in the chilly night.
Stars twinkle softly, a shimmering sight,
Guiding lost spirits with warmth, so bright.

Crisp air carries a sweet, soft tune,
As trees stand guard 'neath the silvered moon.
Frost-kissed petals, a fleeting boon,
Nature's breath held in a peaceful swoon.

Each breath fogs, like a ghost on the air,
Weaving memories in winter's fair.
Embers glisten, a hopeful flare,
In the quiet hours, love's joys prepare.

Through the stillness, a longing sigh,
For warmth in hearts as the world draws nigh.
Winter's emissaries in the sky,
Calling us home, where dreams never die.

Cocooned in blankets, we seek the light,
Chasing the shadows of the endless night.
Embers of hope, we hold them tight,
Till the dawn breaks forth and banishes fright.

Ethereal Glow in a Frozen Dream

In gentle silence, the world transforms,
With cascades of snow in swirling storms.
A canvas of icicles, nature's forms,
Under the moon where mystery warms.

Reflective glimmers as starlight falls,
A hush envelops, the night enthralls.
Colors of twilight through frosty walls,
Echo of laughter, the magic calls.

Footprints linger, a journey begun,
Chasing the shadows and catching the sun.
Ethereal dreams in the night are spun,
As whispers of winter bring hearts to run.

Crystals catch glances in fairy rings,
Wings of enchantment that winter brings.
Embers of joy as the new year sings,
Wrapped in the hush; oh, how time clings!

Fragrant fire mingles with night's embrace,
Recalling the warmth of love's sweet trace.
In frozen dreams, we wander and chase,
A world where the heart finds its true place.

Frosted Orbs Against Night's Canvas

The night sky wears a frosted crown,
Stars like orbs in their silvery gowns.
Each glimmer a story, no need for renown,
Twinkling reminders of dreams that astound.

A hush blankets all in a soft embrace,
While shadows dance in this timeless space.
Frosted orbs whisper of love's grace,
Painting the heavens with delicate lace.

Beneath the heavens, we gather, we share,
In the stillness, find solace, a prayer.
With hope suspended in cool, crisp air,
Wrapped in the magic of winter's care.

The moonlight drapes a silver veil,
As echoes of laughter on soft winds sail.
Frosted orbs shine bright, they prevail,
In the heart of the night, a soothing tale.

With nature's palette, the sky's in bloom,
Carrying whispers of light, dispelling gloom.
A masterpiece crafted in winter's womb,
Where dreams unfold, and love finds room.

Glimmering Lights in the Snowfall

Drifting down as the night unfolds,
Snowflakes shimmer in stories told.
Glimmering lights dance, bright and bold,
Weaving a tapestry, silver and gold.

Candles flicker, a warm embrace,
Lighting the paths, each familiar place.
In the stillness, soft breaths we trace,
As glimmering lights paint the winter's face.

Footsteps crunch on the blanket of white,
Every sound echoing, soft and slight.
Glimmers surround us, pure delight,
In the realm of dreams where hearts take flight.

Nature's theater presents the night,
Sparkling wonders in a glistening sight.
Moments cherished, the world feels right,
Under the glow, love shines so bright.

Beneath the starlit serene expanse,
Life beckons softly, inviting a dance.
Glimmering lights in a timeless romance,
A winter's crystal dream, a fleeting chance.

Whispering Shadows at Dusk

In the twilight's embrace, shadows creep,
Whispering secrets the night will keep.
Leaves dance softly on the cool breeze,
As dusk unfolds with gentle tease.

Veils of purple softly sway,
As daylight bids its sweet farewell play.
Stars awaken, one by one,
While the moon rises, a silver sun.

Crickets sing in rhythmic song,
Nature's choir, where we belong.
Each sound a promise, clear and true,
In the heart of night, we renew.

From the trees, a sigh escapes,
In the hush, the world reshapes.
Mystery wraps each hidden lane,
As dreams begin, unfurling plain.

In shadows deep, whispers glide,
A realm of wonder, chance to bide.
Embrace the night with open heart,
As dawn waits patiently, a new start.

Illuminated Dreams in the Frost

Morning light on frost does gleam,
A canvas pure, a frozen dream.
Each blade of grass, a crystal spear,
Enchanting hearts, drawing near.

Breath hangs heavy in the air,
Whispers of magic linger there.
Each step crunches, soft and light,
Awakening depths of winter's night.

Imprints left in glistening snow,
Stories of wanderers who go.
Branches shimmer with icy lace,
Nature's artistry, a sacred space.

Colors dance in frosty hues,
Pastel skies, the dawn renews.
In this glow, our spirits rise,
Embracing beauty in winter's guise.

With every breath, hope takes flight,
In dreams illuminated, purest light.
We find our way through the cold and gray,
Guided by warmth, come what may.

Glistening Pathways of Light

Under stars, the pathways glimmer,
With each step, our hearts grow warmer.
Guided by soft, ethereal glow,
A world alive, a wondrous show.

Moonbeams dance on dewy leaves,
In the night, nature weaves.
Every whisper, a tale untold,
A journey through mysteries bold.

Along the way, laughter lingers,
Touched by magic, time slips like fingers.
Light reflects off tranquil streams,
In these moments, we chase our dreams.

The night unfolds its velvet cloak,
With every heartbeat, a gentle stroke.
In these pathways lit by stars,
We find ourselves, no matter how far.

Wandering souls on glistening trails,
In awe of life, where wonder prevails.
Each path we tread, a new delight,
Together, we shine in the soft moonlight.

Veiled in Silver and Blue

A shroud of silver blankets the land,
Where moonlit whispers gently stand.
In the stillness, the night unfolds,
Tales of old in silence told.

Deep azure skies hug the night,
Stars flicker softly, twinkling light.
Breezes carry sweet scents anew,
Carving dreams in shades of blue.

Each corner holds a secret song,
In harmony, we dance along.
Voices mingle with the night air,
In this wonder, we find our care.

Twinkling gems in the vast above,
Embracing all with infinite love.
Veils of mystery cloak each hue,
In the still, we seek what's true.

Bathed in silver, softly we roam,
Finding solace far from home.
In night's embrace, we find our way,
Guided by stars till break of day.

The Frosted Embrace of Evening

The air grows still, as shadows creep,
A blanket of frost, a secret to keep.
Moonlight dances on icy streams,
Whispers of night weave through our dreams.

Beneath the trees, in twilight's glow,
Silent secrets in the chill winds blow.
Stars twinkle softly, a distant fire,
Holding our hearts in their cool desire.

Breath turns to mist in the bitter night,
Wrapped in the embrace of soft twilight.
A chill that lingers, yet feels so right,
Enfolding us in nature's gentle sight.

The world is hushed, all sound is bound,
In the frosted embrace, peace can be found.
The moon oversees, with watchful eyes,
As evening unfolds its quiet skies.

In this moment, time stands still,
Nature's calm fills the heart, so full.
With every breath, we feel the sway,
In the frosted embrace, we long to stay.

Celestial Lanterns in the Abyss

In the velvet darkness, stars ignite,
Glow like lanterns in the endless night.
Cosmic whispers call from afar,
Guiding wanderers to where dreams are.

Nebulae swirl in colors bright,
Painting the canvas of ethereal light.
Infinite wonders dance in the space,
Finding solace in the universe's embrace.

From distant galaxies, tales unfold,
Of ancient mysteries, of legends told.
Fleeting moments in the grand design,
Each shining star, a spark divine.

The vast abyss cradles our fears,
Yet, in its beauty, we shed our tears.
For in this darkness, hope takes flight,
As celestial lanterns burn ever bright.

Holding our wishes, they shimmer and plea,
Whispering secrets of what could be.
In the cosmic tapestry, we find our way,
Guided by lanterns that never sway.

Glint of Stars on Frozen Waters

Mirror lakes catch the gleam of night,
Stars glisten softly, a breathtaking sight.
Each reflection, a story untold,
A canvas of wonders, timeless and bold.

The ice sings beneath the silver sheen,
A tranquil silence lingers serene.
Whispers of nature, a gentle song,
Echo through shadows as we drift along.

Footsteps crunch on the frosty ground,
In this quiet beauty, we are found.
Every glint a promise, every twinkle a dream,
In the frozen waters, light dances and beams.

With every breath, the cold air bites,
Yet warmth blooms within on these starry nights.
Together we wander, hearts intertwined,
In the glint of stars, true peace we find.

Nature cradles us in her arms so wide,
On frozen waters, we take in the tide.
Under the cosmos, we watch as we flow,
In the glint of stars, our spirits glow.

Soft Light Across the Cold

Dawn breaks gently, a whisper of gold,
Soft light spills forth to warm the cold.
Each ray a blanket, a tender embrace,
Chasing the shadows, unveiling grace.

The world awakens, a soft sigh released,\nNature
unfurling, the heart finds peace.
Every blade glistens with morning dew,
In the soft light, life starts anew.

Colors bloom as the sun climbs high,
Painting the horizon, the canvas of sky.
Birds take flight, a melodic choir,
In this soft light, our spirits aspire.

Chill of the night fades into the past,
In warmth and beauty, we are steadfast.
Together we breathe in this tranquil sight,
Wrapped in soft light, our souls take flight.

As evening draws near, shadows will hold,
Memories glimmer like treasures of old.
Yet in each moment, we'll carry the glow,
Of soft light across the cold, ever so slow.

Shivering Echoes of Radiance

In whispers soft, the night descends,
Shivering echoes, where light bends.
Stars twinkle gently in the dark,
They guide the lost, like a spark.

Frost-kissed shadows dance in flight,
Reflecting stories of the night.
Each glimmer sings a tune of hope,
Warming hearts, helping us cope.

The cool breeze carries tales untold,
Of quiet dreams and moments bold.
As dawn approaches, hope ignites,
A canvas brushed with morning lights.

In radiant beams, the world awakes,
A tapestry woven with heartaches.
Yet from the pain, beauty shall rise,
Shivering echoes 'neath vast skies.

So let us cherish each fleeting ray,
In shining memories, we shall stay.
Through all the trials that we face,
We find in darkness, a gentle grace.

Illuminating Peace in Silent Fields

Beneath the hush of twilight's glow,
Silent fields where soft winds blow.
Whispers pass through blades of grass,
Carrying secrets that time won't pass.

Golden hues paint the gentle earth,
In quiet moments, we find our worth.
Each leaf a story, each bloom a sigh,
They remind us how to dream high.

The moonlight bathes the world in peace,
Inviting our worries to quietly cease.
Nature wraps us in a warm embrace,
In every shadow, we find grace.

Stars sprinkle joy upon our dreams,
Guiding us through the soft moonbeams.
In this silence, our spirits soar,
Finding solace forevermore.

So let us wander these peaceful lanes,
Where love lingers and softly remains.
In silent fields, our hearts take flight,
Illuminating peace through the night.

Fantasies in Winter's Embrace

In winter's arms, the world grows still,
Fantasies dance with a snowy thrill.
Dreams unfold like flakes of white,
Whirling softly in the night.

Crisp air whispers tales so sweet,
Every heartbeat feels complete.
Footsteps crunch on frosty ground,
Magical moments all around.

Stars above in a velvet sky,
Watch as the world holds a sigh.
Each breath clouds in the chilly air,
Fleeting moments beyond compare.

Slowly drifting through this scene,
Winter's grace is a soft routine.
Each glance reveals a shimmered dream,
In the silence, our hearts gleam.

So let us linger in winter's sway,
Where joy and peace find their way.
In fantasies woven from the frost,
We discover beauty, never lost.

Frosted Stories from the Heart of Ice

In frozen realms where shadows dwell,
Frosted stories weave a spell.
Each fragment glistens in the light,
A tale of warmth in the cold night.

Crystalline breath of snowflakes fall,
Softly, they whisper and softly call.
With every flake, a memory spins,
Of love once lost and where it begins.

Through icy branches, whispers flow,
Tales of the past beneath the snow.
Nature holds secrets, hidden tight,
In the heart of winter's silent night.

Glimmers of laughter, echoes of tears,
Remind us gently through the years.
Frosted moments, pure and bright,
Guiding us home through the icy night.

So let us listen to winter's song,
In the heart of ice, where we belong.
These frosted stories, forever remain,
In every heartbeat, joy and pain.

Dappled Radiance Under the Moon

In the hush of night, soft beams play,
Silver shadows dance, a fleeting sway.
Whispers of silver paint the trees,
While dreams entwine like fragrant breeze.

Glowing orbs in a velvet sky,
Glimmers of magic, clouds drift by.
Moonlit paths where secrets dwell,
In dappled light, all is well.

Gentle light on the quiet ground,
Serenading hearts with a tranquil sound.
Each ray a brushstroke of the divine,
Unfolding stories in silence, entwined.

Night's embrace cradles the day,
Casting a charm that won't fade away.
In this realm of shadows and gleam,
Life whispers softly, a tender dream.

Caught in spell's weave, lost in time,
Where every verse unmasks a rhyme.
In dappled radiance, souls take flight,
Under the gaze of the full moon's light.

The Celestial Tapestry Aglow

Stars weave a tapestry, pure and bright,
Threads of stardust, a captivating sight.
Beneath the heavens, hearts intertwine,
In the cosmic dance, we align.

Colors flicker in a boundless sea,
A galaxy's song, an eternal decree.
Nebulas swirl, a painter's delight,
Whispers of wonder glitter in the night.

Constellations guard tales of old,
Stories of love, of courage bold.
In the silent abyss, we find our place,
Lost within the vastness of space.

Every twinkle a promise, a dream,
In the celestial glow, shadows gleam.
We gather beneath the luminous dome,
In this vibrant cosmos, we call home.

A symphony of light fills the skies,
Painting our thoughts as we realize.
Together we wander, hearts in tow,
In the celestial tapestry aglow.

Enigma of the Frozen Glow

Upon the lake, a shimmering sheen,
Bound in ice, a crystalline dream.
Cold whispers breathe through frozen air,
Mysteries dwell, silent and rare.

Frosted branches, a delicate lace,
Nature's art in a still embrace.
Glimmers reflect like stars at play,
In the soft hush of the winter day.

Each step we take crunches so loud,
Breaking the calm of the winter shroud.
In this enigma, we pause to see,
The beauty of stillness, wild and free.

Shadows drawn in the moonlit embrace,
Nature's secret, a tender grace.
As night cloaks the world, we exhale slow,
Embracing the magic of the frozen glow.

Here in the still, a tale unfolds,
Of warmth found within the bitter cold.
With each heartbeat, the silence flows,
In the enigma where the frozen glows.

Frost's Lullaby Under Starlit Skies

In the cradle of night, a lullaby sings,
Frost lingers soft on gentle wings.
Crickets serenade the sleeping trees,
Nature whispers sweetly, carried by the breeze.

Stars flicker softly in their soft nest,
Bathing the world in a tranquil rest.
Every sparkle, a soothing embrace,
Painting dreams on the earth's quiet face.

Moonlight spills through the silvery veil,
Guiding lost hearts on a dreamy trail.
Under this canopy, worries take flight,
Wrapped in the arms of the cool, soft night.

Each breath a whisper, each sigh a song,
In the chorus of night where we all belong.
Frost crowns the land as the shadows play,
In sweet serenades of night's ballet.

Dreamers gather in this peaceful space,
Finding solace in the starlit grace.
With frost's lullaby, the world is aglow,
In the quiet magic where love can grow.

Chill-Kissed Sentinels of the Dark

Tall trees whisper secrets, cold and still,
Guardians of dreams beneath the moonlit chill.
Branches stretch like arms to hold the night,
In their embrace, shadows blend with light.

Stars twinkle softly, watching from above,
Nature's quiet heartbeat, a pulse of love.
Frost paints the world in glistening white,
While the chill-kissed sentinels shun the light.

Beneath their boughs, the earth seems to sigh,
Wrapped in blankets of silence, speaks the sky.
With every whisper, the dark becomes deep,
And the secrets of night lull the world to sleep.

In the stillness, thoughts drift like clouds,
Veiled in tranquility, mystery shrouds.
The watchful trees, with roots intertwined,
Stand firm as witnesses, ancient and blind.

Among the shadows, the breeze softly plays,
A haunting melody in twilight's haze.
Chill-kissed sentinels guard the night air,
While the world around dreams without a care.

Celestial Crystals Adrift in Winter

Winter's breath blankets the ground in white,
Crystals glisten softly, catching the light.
Each flake a wonder, a work of art,
Dancing on breezes, a magical start.

Under the twilight, they shimmer and glow,
Silent sentinels whisper their flow.
From branches to rooftops, a sight to behold,
Celestial wonders, more precious than gold.

The world turns to silver, with each gentle fall,
Nature's soft canvas, painted for all.
The chill in the air, a reminder so clear,
Winter's embrace, cold but sincere.

Stars sparkle brightly, reflecting the scene,
Crystals a-glimmer, like dreams yet unseen.
They drift in the silence, soft landings beneath,
A world filled with magic, wrapped up in peace.

Celestial crystals, in their soft descent,
Whisper to winter, their sweet lament.
Dancing through moonlight, a season so grand,
In the heart of the night, we together will stand.

Luminous Crystals in a Quiet World

In the quiet night, the crystals gleam,
Soft fragments of light, like a shattered dream.
They scatter and glisten, so fragile, yet bright,
Painting the shadows with colors of night.

Each twinkle a promise, a wish made anew,
Luminous whispers that carry the dew.
In the stillness, they sing of forgotten lore,
Helplessly drawn to the heart of the core.

Beneath the vast heavens, under the star's gaze,
Crystals drift slowly, lost in a haze.
Every flicker a dance, an elegant sway,
Guiding the dreamers who wander and stray.

In the calm of the evening, solace unfolds,
Luminous wonders are timid yet bold.
The softest of currents, the gentlest touch,
In this quiet world, can mean so much.

Let the glow lead our hearts through the dark,
A beacon of hope, like a luminous spark.
In the depths of the silence, we find our way,
With crystals of light, together we'll stay.

Shining Hope in a Winter's Tale

When winter embraces the earth once more,
Hope shimmers brightly, a flame to explore.
In the heart of the cold, where the shadows reside,
A shining light blossoms, a spark deep inside.

With each falling flake, a story unfolds,
The warmth of the heart, more precious than gold.
Beneath icy layers, the ember still breathes,
In the stillness of night, a promise it weaves.

Branches heavily laden with crystalline lace,
Mirrored reflections of beauty and grace.
The world starts to glow under moon's gentle sway,
As shining hope lingers, guiding our way.

Whispers of winter sing soft in the trees,
A tale of resilience, carried on breeze.
With each step we take on this snow-blanketed path,
Shining hope sparkles, igniting our wrath.

So let the world twirl in its magical dance,
With winters that chill, yet bring forth romance.
In the arms of the night, let our hearts intertwine,
For in every harsh season, the spark of hope shines.

Chill Embraces Glimmer

In the stillness of the night,
A soft glow begins to rise.
Whispers float on frosty air,
Each twinkle a sweet surprise.

Silver shadows dance around,
Casting dreams upon the ground.
Crisp and cool, the world aglow,
As the stars begin to bow.

Gentle breezes brush our skin,
Inviting warmth from deep within.
In this tranquil, gleaming space,
We find solace, find our place.

Glittering flakes start to fall,
Nature's crystal, pure and tall.
Embracing us with every touch,
As the chill inspires so much.

Underneath this starry dome,
We feel the chill, yet call it home.
In the glimmer, hearts unite,
Wrapped in peace, sweet and bright.

Twinkling Veils of Ice

Veils of ice, they softly gleam,
In the moonlight's gentle beam.
Nature dons her frosty dress,
Whispering secrets of finesse.

Every flake a story told,
Glistening like strands of gold.
Through the branches, light cascades,
Creating magic in the shades.

Frozen whispers fill the air,
Laughter dances everywhere.
Golden twinkles, shy yet bright,
Painting dreams in winter's night.

Crisp and clear, the world stands still,
Heartbeats echo, time to thrill.
Wrapped in warmth beneath the sky,
Twinkling veils make spirits fly.

In this moment, so divine,
Underneath the stars that shine.
Ice and light, a sweet embrace,
In this winter's sacred space.

Glistening Lights in the Silence

In the heart of winter's glow,
Glistening lights align in rows.
Calm descends like gentle snow,
Whispering secrets we both know.

Each flicker tells a tale unseen,
Softly basking in the serene.
The world outside, so hushed and still,
Encased in beauty, warmth, and chill.

Silver threads weave through the dark,
Illuminating every spark.
Frosty air, a breath divine,
In silence, our hearts quietly entwine.

Every corner glimmers bright,
In the tender, tranquil night.
Waves of warmth in icy graces,
Lighting up our hidden places.

In this silence, find your peace,
As the glistening lights increase.
Let the winter's magic flow,
In soft shadows, let love grow.

Ethereal Beacons Through the Cold

Through the cold, ethereal glow,
Beacons of light begin to show.
A celestial dance unfolds,
Guiding hearts, as evening holds.

Stars above like diamonds shine,
Illuminating paths divine.
Each step we take, hope ignites,
In the peaceful, chilly nights.

Frosty whispers graze our cheeks,
Nature speaks, as silence speaks.
Gentle warmth entwines our hands,
As we traverse these silver lands.

Candles flickering in the breeze,
Carving shadows through the trees.
Ethereal beacons, soft yet bold,
Whisper tales of warmth untold.

In the night, the world stands still,
Wrapped in beauty, hearts to fill.
Together, we'll embrace the cold,
As ethereal stories unfold.

Ethereal Sparks Beneath the Cold

In twilight whispers, secrets dance,
Softly glowing, the night enchants.
Each breath we take, a shivered sigh,
As fleeting dreams awake and fly.

Crystal shards beneath our feet,
Echoes of warmth in the night's heartbeat.
Frosted branches weave a tale,
Of winter's grace, a gentle veil.

In shadows cast by celestial lights,
Magic stirs in the wintry nights.
The air, alive with shimmering grace,
As ethereal sparks begin to trace.

Hearts entwined in the icy glow,
Lost in wonder, time moves slow.
Underneath the stars so bright,
We find solace in the tranquil night.

As dawn approaches, shadows wane,
Yet in our souls, the warmth remains.
Ethereal sparks, a fleeting bliss,
In chilly air, a tender kiss.

Shadowy Flickers in Calm

Amidst the night, soft shadows play,
Flickering lights that gently sway.
Whispers echo through the trees,
In harmony with the cold breeze.

Moonlit paths invite the lost,
In stillness, there's a hidden cost.
Each flicker tells a tale of yore,
Of moments passed and dreams of more.

Beneath the calm, a heartbeat lies,
Shadowy flickers, hidden sighs.
The world in slumber, holding tight,
To secrets wrapped in the velvet night.

Within the hush, where spirits roam,
Flickering shadows find their home.
Unseen voices call us near,
In the silence, truths appear.

As dawn breaks forth, shadows retreat,
Yet in our hearts, they leave a heat.
Flickers fade but memories stay,
In the calm, where dreams will play.

Luminous Secrets of the Frozen Terrain

Beneath a veil of frost and snow,
Lies a world of secrets, soft and slow.
Luminous glimmers in the night,
Painting stories with purest light.

Each flake a whisper, soft and bright,
Carving patterns in the still night.
Frozen terrain, a canvas white,
Where dreams awaken, taking flight.

In stillness, one can hear the call,
Of crystalline wonders that befall.
Luminous secrets in the eaves,
Entwined with hope on the frosty leaves.

As stars twinkle, a guiding flame,
Unlocking paths we cannot name.
In every corner, a story lies,
Awaiting the dawn to realize.

Through the chill, our spirits warm,
Embracing the magic, the perfect form.
Luminous secrets, the night's delight,
In frozen ground, we find our light.

Stars Weaving Under a Blanket of Ice

Beneath the blanket, silence keeps,
Stars weave tales while the whole world sleeps.
Glittering threads of radiant hope,
In the vastness, they learn to cope.

Each twinkling light, a story told,
Of dreams suspended in the cold.
Crystalline dreams dance and sway,
Guiding lost hearts along the way.

Under ice, they find their grace,
Stars weave through the night's embrace.
In frosty air, echoes arise,
From the canvas of starry skies.

Each shimmer holds the promise bright,
Of tomorrow born from this night.
Wrapped in ice, yet hearts remain,
Awash in warmth despite the pain.

As dawn approaches, the magic fades,
Yet in our souls, the beauty wades.
Stars weaving stories, bold and free,
Under the blanket, eternally.

Enchanted Light in Chilly Embrace

Through frosty air, the whispers gleam,
A silver glow, like a waking dream.
Soft shadows dance, in twilight's hand,
Embracing warmth, in winter's land.

Gentle flurries twirl and sway,
Emboldened by a golden ray.
Illuminated paths begin to glow,
As stars above start their evening show.

Beneath the trees, the fireflies play,
Their flickering lights chase dusk away.
Each flick, a promise, in the night,
A world transformed, in enchanted light.

In snowy drifts, the echoes rise,
Where whispers meet the starlit skies.
A touch of magic, cool and bright,
In chilly embrace, we find delight.

The moonlit hours soon intertwine,
As dreams of warmth begin to shine.
Embraced by night, the heart will find,
A canvas vast, where love is kind.

Candlelight's Kiss in Winter's Air

Candlelight's touch upon the skin,
Warms the quiet, where dreams begin.
Flickers dance, in shadows' play,
A soft embrace, for the end of day.

Windows frost with a crystalline hue,
As night descends, we gather too.
In the glow, hearts intertwine,
A moment held, so pure, divine.

Silent whispers of snowflakes drift,
While candle flames give a gentle lift.
Each flicker sings a lullaby sweet,
In winter's air, where lovers meet.

Beneath the stars, so bright above,
We find our warmth in the glow of love.
In each breath, the chill dissipates,
As candlelight's kiss, softly awaits.

The world outside, a wonderland,
While here we hold each other's hand.
In the warmth, the cold cannot stay,
As night unfolds, and dreams play.

Dancing Fires in a Frozen Hall

Fires flicker in the frozen night,
Dancing shadows, a mystical sight.
Wood crackles with a symphony's cheer,
In this hall where warmth draws near.

Vibrant flames twist with a magical grace,
Illuminating each familiar face.
Laughter echoes off icy walls,
As we celebrate in winter's halls.

The chill outside can't steal our glow,
As the fire flickers, our spirits flow.
In the heart of the night, we gather round,
While outside, the world is softly bound.

Sheltered here from the biting air,
With a drink in hand, love we share.
The warmth of hearts, the light of fire,
In frozen repose, our souls aspire.

So let the winds continue to howl,
In this cherished place, we make our vow.
For as long as the night takes its toll,
Dancing fires will warm every soul.

Shining Reflections on Crystal Lakes

Beneath the moon, the waters gleam,
Crystal lakes hold a silver dream.
Reflections dance with the night's soft sigh,
As stars above twinkle in reply.

The softest ripples break the peace,
In their embrace, time holds its cease.
A hush envelops the world around,
In nature's stillness, serenity found.

Ice crowns adorn the edges there,
Framing the beauty with delicate care.
Nature whispers in the crisp, cool air,
While dreams glide upon the water's glare.

In this tranquil place, we float and sway,
As shimmering lights invite us to stay.
The lake, a mirror, of what once was,
Reflects our hopes and love's gentle pause.

With every glance, new stories unfold,
Of whispered secrets, both young and old.
On crystal lakes, where heartstrings play,
Shining reflections guide our way.

Serenity Wrapped in Glowing White

In silence deep, the world unfolds,
A blanket pure, where peace enfolds.
Footprints left in whispered snow,
Where gentle winds of stillness blow.

The sky a canvas, soft and bright,
With hues that dance in soft twilight.
Each breath a chill, a moment's pause,
Nature's heart, in silent applause.

A spark of warmth in winter's chill,
A tranquil grace, a heart to fill.
Here time stands still, as dreams awaken,
In glowing white, my cares forsaken.

The hour glows with soft delight,
Crystalline shards in tranquil night.
Beneath the stars, my spirit soars,
Wrapped in peace, forevermore.

Each flake a promise, pure and bright,
In this serene, enchanted light.
With every breath, I find my way,
In glowing white, I long to stay.

Sparkling Echoes of Nature's Light

In the meadow, dewdrops gleam,
Nature whispers, soft as a dream.
Sunbeams dance on leaves so green,
A tapestry of vibrant sheen.

Birdsongs echo, pure delight,
Harmonies in morning's light.
Every rustle, every sigh,
Nature's melody fills the sky.

Mountains rise in stately grace,
Framing life in timeless space.
With every breeze, the world does sing,
To the rhythm that nature brings.

Rivers shimmer, winding free,
Reflecting shadows, joy, and glee.
In every drop, a story flows,
Of sparkling echoes, beauty grows.

The twilight brings a golden hue,
Stars emerge, the night renewed.
In the silence, hearts take flight,
Sparkling echoes of nature's light.

Soft Radiance of Winter's Grasp

The world adorned in quiet white,
Hushed beneath the moon's soft light.
With every breath, the frosty air,
Whispers secrets, pure and rare.

Icicles hang like crystal dreams,
Glistening in the silver beams.
A blanket wraps the trees so tall,
In winter's grasp, we hear the call.

Snowflakes twirl in graceful flight,
Each one a gift, a pure delight.
A tapestry of peace and grace,
In this soft, radiant embrace.

Footprints fade on the silver ground,
In quietude, the heart is found.
With winter's touch, I come alive,
In this soft glow, I thrive.

The evenings hum with peaceful light,
As stars awaken, shining bright.
With every moment, love can last,
In soft radiance of winter's grasp.

Frost-Cast Dreams in the Night

In the stillness, cold and clear,
Frosty whispers draw me near.
The moonlight weaves a silver thread,
Where dreams take shape, and hopes are fed.

Shadows dance on fields of white,
In the silence of the night.
Each crystal glows with magic's kiss,
A moment's pause, a fleeting bliss.

The world asleep in a gentle hold,
Stories of the night unfold.
Beneath the stars, my spirit flies,
As frost-cast dreams kiss the skies.

Fires crackle, warmth inside,
While winter's charm, we must abide.
In every glimmer, tales remain,
Of frost and dreams, a sweet refrain.

Awakened hearts in the quiet night,
Find solace in the soft moonlight.
Frost-cast dreams in stillness gleam,
A world reborn, a timeless dream.

Milton Keynes UK
Ingram Content Group UK Ltd.
UKHW010229111224
452348UK00011B/617